Lost Bar Harbor

Lost Bar Harbor

G. W. Helfrich
& Gladys O'Neil

For Lisa
— thanks for her
efforts
Bill Helfrich

photographs from the collection of
the Bar Harbor Historical Society

Down East Books • Camden, Maine

Copyright © 1982 by G. W. Helfrich and Gladys O'Neil
ISBN 0-89272-142-1
Library of Congress Catalog Card Number 82-71103
Design: Karen Searls
Composition: The Offset House
Printed in the United States of America

Down East Books, Camden, Maine 04843

10   9   8   7   6

To the memory of
Mrs. John Dewitt Peltz
who loved the island
and
to Lisa,
who was born in Bar Harbor

Contents

Acknowledgments

An unassuming little museum housed in the basement of the Jesup Memorial Library, the Bar Harbor Historical Society is the proper repository for all things relating to lost Bar Harbor. Sine qua non for the scholar, for the casual traveler possessed of an intelligent curiosity, there is no better place to while away a rainy afternoon. In any kind of weather, the museum offers an interesting and instructive refuge from the tourist hordes without.

Most of the photographs of cottages reproduced here are from the museum, but there are, sadly, still gaps in the collection, and thanks are due to the following for their generosity in furnishing photographs: to Stetson Carter for Chatwold; to Thomas Dillon of Philadelphia for Wingwood House; to the Bar Harbor Club for the Bar Harbor Swimming Club; to Mrs. Lewis Garland for Reef Point, both house and garden; to Major Ogden McCagg of Stonington, Connecticut, for Woodlands; to the Kebo Valley Golf Club for the Kebo Valley Club House and Mrs. James MacLeod for Mizzentop; to Mrs. R. Amory Thorndike for The Craigs and The Eyrie; to John B. Walls for the DeGregoire Hotel; and to Down East Magazine for Edgemere and Ban-Y-Byrn.

Others who were helpful in various ways were Gayle Arnold and Charles Arnold; Earl Brechlin; Theodore Falkenstrom; Arthur Hubbard and Judy Johnson of Images; Claire Lambert of the Jesup Memorial Library; and Katherine Richards.

For permission to quote from *The Shingle Style and the Stick Style*, our thanks go to Yale University Press and author Vincent J. Scully, Jr.

Illustrations in the introduction are reprinted from *Bar Harbor Days*, by Mrs. Burton Harrison, Harper & Brothers, 1887; and from *The Summer School of Philosophy at Mt. Desert*, by J.A. Mitchell, Henry Holt & Co., 1881.

Portland and Bar Harbor
March 1982

G.W.H.
G. O'N.

HORSE SHOW AT ROBIN HOOD PARK

Introduction

"The growth of the American watering-place," wrote E. L. Godkin nearly a century ago, "seems to be as much regulated by law as the growth of asparagus or strawberries, and is almost as easy to foretell." Godkin had Bar Harbor in mind when he wrote those words, and his theory of resort evolution has since been adopted and embellished by every historian of the island from George Street to Samuel Eliot Morison.

Godkin's scenario goes like this: The first summer visitors are artists and naturalists, well-to-do clergymen and their families, college professors and students — in short, people with leisure time. They board with the natives, accept the plain and homely fare, and find their pleasure in the open air, in sketching, fishing, hiking, boating, or in simply admiring the scenery. At the end of the summer, they depart, and their hosts, counting their money, conclude that taking in boarders is an excellent thing. Boarders return year after year, become old boarders, and get the best rooms. The proprietor soon finds it necessary to enlarge his dining room, perhaps add a wing, and offer his guests fried mutton and potatoes to supplement the usual diet of herring and beans. He begins to advertise, and solicits testimonials from ministers and editors. His success, of course, does not go unnoticed by his neighbors, who are quick to follow his example. New boarding houses spring up. Small boarding houses grow into big boarding houses, then into hotels with added refinements such as guest registers. Then the hotels grow larger and larger, until the day arrives when Bar Harbor has become famous — and crowded.

But long before this stage, the first cottagers appeared. They were, in most cases, especially in the early years, former boarders who, impressed by the tonic air and the grandeur of the scenery, decided to buy a lot and build on it. The first cottages were simple single-story structures, often referred to as huts or shanties, and their owners continued to take their meals in the hotels. Inevitably, more and grander "cottages" and "Italian villas" were built, with carefully manicured lawns, private tennis courts, footmen in livery, and other plutocratic excrescences.* The now lowly boarder soon found himself a trespasser on every desirable site from the Ovens to Great Head. For the democratic Godkin, who apotheosized the early boarder as a man of plain living and high thinking (stimulated, he thought, "through an exclusively fish diet"), the dislodgement of the boarder by the cottager was the "great summer tragedy of American life." Godkin died in 1905, before the deluge.

The original summer people were, of course, the Indians, the Abnakis belonging to the Algonkian language group. After spring planting of corn, beans, and pumpkins, leaving the old folks and the dogs behind, they went

---

*According to Cleveland Amory, the word *cottage* was used originally to denote the small buildings that were built around the large hotels to house the overflow of guests. In time, these cottages became more desirable than the rooms in the hotels, and when the patrons began to build their own homes, they kept the word *and* the social cachet it had acquired.

down to the sea in birch-bark canoes. Arriving at Pemetic ("range of mountains"), they set up camp near tidal flats. Here the men fished, placed weirs to trap eels, and harpooned porpoises, while their squaws dug, shucked, and dried clams, gathered roots, berries and sweet grass, and peeled birch bark to make baskets. At the end of the summer, they returned to their villages for the harvest.

These early idylls came to an end with the English settlement; the first English settlers made no mention of Indians in the neighborhood. Their subsequent history on Mount Desert Island replicates their history elsewhere. Small numbers of Indians camped at the foot of Bridge Street, opposite Bar Island. An 1881 guidebook states that the "most accessible shell heaps are on the eastern end of Bar Island and at Hull's Cove." Banished for a while from the island, the Indians returned to a marshy field known as Squaw Hollow (in back of the present-day athletic field). With the coming of the Village Improvement Association, they were forced to retreat still further to an area along a back road. In the early years of this century they were described as living in tents and tarpaper and bark shanties, reduced to selling basketwork, toy canoes, bows and arrows, and moccasins.

Although Thomas Doughty of Philadelphia probably painted on the island about 1836 — his composite *Mount Desert Lighthouse* was engraved in N. P. Willis's *American Scenery* in 1838 — the visit of his pupil Thomas Cole in the late summer of 1844 was a significant event in island history. On September 3, 1844 — we have the exact date from his diary — Cole, armed with sketchbook, drove across the island to stay at the Lynam Homestead near Schooner Head. Cole is generally considered to be the founder of the Hudson River School of painters, a rather loose geographical designation for a group of landscape painters and their grandiose style of depicting mountains, clouds, dramatic outcroppings of rock, and dwarfed fir against skies usually filled with sweeping yellows and reds. Other members of the school followed: Frederick Church, Thomas Birch, William Hart. It was Church and his fellow artists who gave names to Eagle Lake, the Beehive, Echo Lake, and the Porcupines.

Church, the most accomplished member of the school, may properly be called the founder of the Bar Harbor summer colony. Church boarded from 1850 on with Albert Higgins in Bar Harbor (Fitz Hugh Lane, the founding figure of luminism, was also there that summer) and returned several times during the next few years. His exhibition in 1850 at the New York Art Union, and one in 1852 in which he showed *Fog Off Mount Desert Island* and *Beacon Off Mount Desert Island*, did much to publicize the island. In 1855 Church and his sister were among the party of twenty-six led by New York lawyer Charles Tracy, whose daughter Frances was to marry J. P. Morgan the Elder.* Tracy,

---

*Contrary to popular legend, Morgan I was never a cottager. At the turn of the century, however, he spent a part of every summer on board his yacht, the *Corsair*, or at the cottage of his daughter, Mrs. Herbert Satterlee. Occasionally he would come ashore for stays of varying length at the homes of *two* ladies on High Street.

who may be considered Bar Harbor's social pioneer, kept a log of the voyage. They left by boat July 30, 1855, went by rail from Fall River to Boston, then by boat to Tremont via Rockland, arriving at noon August 1. After a hearty meal of fish chowder, clam chowder, ham, mutton, peas, new potatoes, pies, puddings, and French preserves, the party went up Somes Sound to Somes's house. A piano arrived by sailboat the next day, the "first ever sounded in Somesville." For the next month, they hiked and fished, played parlor games, and made frequent trips to Schooner Head and Lynam's. Tracy noted that the island bore little farm produce other than hay, oats, buckwheat, corn, barley, and potatoes. "Commerce and fisheries are the business of everybody here. . . . The inhabitants seem to be in a comfortable state between riches and poverty," and they "did not pry."

It was a watershed year for Bar Harbor. Tobias Roberts, who kept a small store, opened the Agamont House, Bar Harbor's first hotel. The first to sign the register were F. E. Church and J. F. Kensett of New York. The date was July 5, 1855.

If anyone deserves to be called the founding father of Bar Harbor's tourist industry, it is Tobias Roberts. In addition to his hotel, he also built a primitive wharf at the foot of Main Street, and in 1857 the steamboat *Rockland*, which had stopped at Southwest Harbor earlier in the 1850s, added Bar Harbor to its run. Steamboat service was interrupted by the Civil War, during which the *Rockland* was lost, but it was resumed in 1868 with the *Ulysses* and the Portland, Mount Desert & Machias Steamboat Company's *Lewiston*, commanded by Captain Charles Deering, who had built Bar Harbor's second hotel, the Deering House, in 1858.

These developments were not adventitious. The herring fisheries and coasting trades were declining, the hills had been stripped of the last trees suitable for sawing, and the thin soil of the farms was exhausted. In the summer of 1858, a New York journalist named Robert Carter sailed Down East with two lively companions aboard the sloop *Helena*. The sailors spent two or three days in Bar Harbor. Carter noted, "Of late years, Mount Desert has become a favorite resort for artists and summer loungers. . . . The 'forest primeval' has been cut down." Carter's amusing dispatches, which were later published in book form, appeared originally in Horace Greeley's New York *Tribune*, then the most influential newspaper in America. Carter's account was probably the first description of the island to appear in print.

At least two distinguished figures visited the island in the 1860s. The first was S. Weir Mitchell, Philadelphia physician and man of letters, who wrote to his sister about 1863:

> Mount Desert is a jolly place, twenty miles long, ten broad;
> mountains in the middle; eight lakes between them; sea wall
> all around island, sometimes five feet high, sometimes eight
> hundred. Lots of caves full of pools; pools full of anemones.
> Surf breaks over said rocks considerably. . . . Fare, ahem! $1.50
> a day, potatoes and mutton, mutton and potatoes; clam

chowder, fish chowder; plum pie, which means blueberry ditto. However, we had a trunkful of potted things, pickles, champagne, whiskey, chocolate, etc. A day's board represents the money value of an acre of land at East Eden.*

In September 1864, the Swiss-born Harvard naturalist Louis Agassiz arrived to collect specimens of rock. One day he noticed he was being watched intently by a young workman from a nearby blacksmith's shop, who offered to lend a hand with a crowbar in breaking off a sample. Agassiz was astonished when the man refused his offer of recompense for his help. His name, which ought to be preserved for posterity, was William Abbott of Tremont.

By the end of the 1860s, the Agamont and the Deering House (now owned by Charles Higgins, one of four hotel-owning Higgins brothers) were joined by Captain James Hamor's Hamor House and A. F. Higgins's Harbor House (both built in 1864), David Rodick's Rodick House (1866), and the Bay View House (1868) of Messrs. Hamor and Young. In 1869 four more hotels were opened, and four were under construction. That August the Ellsworth *American* reported that of 125 passengers who arrived on the *Lewiston* on August 4, 50 were obliged to return because of a lack of accommodations. At year's end, in summing up the season just passed, the *American* said that one-half million feet of lumber had been brought into Bar Harbor that summer, and that the sound of hammer and saw was heard from dawn to dusk. Three cottages — the first was Alpheus Hardy's Birch Point — were built that year, and an eighteen-acre lot at Cromwell Harbor with a small house sold for $1,500!

By 1872 there were fifteen hotels, including the Atlantic and the Newport, and the prosperous hotel era, which extended into the mid-1880s, was fairly launched. A writer for *Harper's Magazine*, surveying the scene at this time, wrote that most "visitors to Mount Desert, even the prosaic folk, go prepared to enjoy the picturesque, the beautiful, the sublime." The accent was on youth. During the day, parties of several persons, ladies and gentlemen, started off on walking expeditions of five, ten, or fifteen miles. "There is a vigorous, sensible, healthy feeling in all they do, and not a bit of that over-dressed, pretentious, nonsensical, unhealthy sentimentality which may be found at other places." The "other places" were Long Branch and Newport.

The excursionists returned at day's end to conditions that were primitive, at least to *Harper's* sniffish correspondent. The beds, stuffed with corn husks, were hard and lumpy, the rooms scantily furnished. Echoing Mitchell's opinion of the local cuisine, he wrote: "When one sits down at a Mount Desert table, the memories of Parker's beefsteak, or Delmonico's Poulet à l'Espagnol, to say nothing of the luxuries of the home table, come thronging sumptuously before him to banish whatever little appetite remains. When people cook and eat food of this wretched description, there must be something wrong in their moral condition. . . . The unfortunate creatures who cook at these places will

---

*From Burr, A. R. *Weir Mitchell*. New York: Duffield, 1929.

make bread with about equal quantities of flour and saleratus; they are determined to fry meat rather than roast, broil, boil, or stew it." He conceded, however, that this "diet is perhaps satisfying to the intellectual Bostonian."

With the coming of the 1880s the hotel era was in full swing. The chief pleasures of the rusticators — still unconventional, youthful, and not given to elaborate apparel — were boating, tramping, sketching, and doing something called "rocking," which is variously described as scrambling over slippery intertidal rocks in search of the seashore's flora and fauna, or, as depicted in Constance Cary Harrison's *Bar Harbor Days*, simply lounging about on granite ledges — in pairs, of course. Picnics at Jordan Pond were popular. This excursion was made by buckboard to Eagle Lake, which was crossed by steamer; the party continued by foot over the "carry" to Jordan Pond, where rowboats were waiting. Supper was had on the grass near the farmer's house, which later became better known as the Jordan Pond House.

The few private homes were still extremely simple and nearly everyone lived either in the hotels or in little wooden cottages without kitchens. Those in the latter had to go to one of the hotels for their food and were known as "mealers" if they were near enough to walk, and "hauled mealers" if they had to be fetched with a cart.

The sea was still the highroad to Mount Desert Island. The steamers *Lewiston* and *City of Richmond* left Portland on alternate weekdays upon arrival of trains from Boston. A third steamer, the *Mount Desert*, met the Bangor steamer at Rockland. In 1881, with five thousand mouths to feed at the height of the season, a second wharf was under construction. In 1884 visitors began to arrive by Maine Central Railroad at a railhead at Hancock Point; they were then conveyed the eight miles across Frenchman Bay by ferry. Within three years rail traffic had trebled, and the Maine Central was carrying over thirty thousand passengers to and from the island. Another ten thousand were carried by steamers.

At the end of the 1882 season, the Mount Desert *Herald*, in a poignant editorial, observed that cottage life had become distinct from hotel life. Cottagers were now entertaining one another with musicales, suppers, dinners, and dances. "Germans" (cotillions) and hops were supplanting picnics, tramps, rows, and climbs. Social emulation had set in, with its attendant rivalries and jealousies. Transients — that is, hotel guests — were at a loss. They sat and rocked on the piazzas and left disappointed. Bar Harbor was becoming fashionable.

In a fictional narrative of America's most fashionable watering places that was serialized in *Harper's* in 1886, Charles Dudley Warner, chronicler of the Gilded Age, wrote:

> For many years . . . [Bar Harbor] had been frequented by people who have more fondness for nature than they have money, and who were willing to put up with wretched accommodations and enjoyed a mild sort of 'roughing it'. . . . The notion spread that it was the finest sanitorium in America

"ROCKING," AT MOUNT DESERT.

for flirtations; and as trade is said to follow the flag, so in this case real estate speculation rioted in the wake of beauty and fashion.

Land values on the island were soaring. Whereas in 1876 Fernald's Point had been offered with considerable other real estate for $3,500, by 1888 the owners refused $60,000 for the Point alone. Streets were laid, sewers constructed (in 1873 Bar Harbor survived an outbreak of typhoid), and water (from Eagle Lake) and electric lights were introduced.

SOME FUNDAMENTAL CONSIDERATIONS,
as realized on Rodick's Piazza.

The highwater mark of the hotel era was reached in 1888, when eighteen hotels accommodated upward of twenty-five hundred guests at the peak of the season. The expanded Rodick House, now the largest hotel in Maine, housed six hundred guests, and rooms had to be reserved two years in advance. The other principal hostelries were the Grand Central (350), the West End (320), and the St. Sauveur (175). The "Fish Pond," a large room at the Rodick House, was *the* meeting place for couples, and all contemporary accounts agree that Bar Harbor afforded young unmarried couples an unusual degree of freedom in that heavily chaperoned age. Other pastimes that were supplanting walking and talking were boat races, bowling, and tennis.

The wharf was alive with vehicles and tooters for the hotels when F. Marion Crawford arrived in Bar Harbor in the early 1890s. Proceeding up Main Street from the wharf past a congeries of tintype artists, Chinese laundries, and hawkers of sandwiches and temperance beverages, Crawford observed, "There are now a number of cottages, most of them simple, with here and there a few that are elaborate, and about a dozen hotels, three or four of which seem to be always full and prosperous [probably the Newport, St. Sauveur, and the "dainty and refined" Malvern]. . . . Others have frankly given up the game and are permanently closed and for sale." Among the latter was the moribund Rodick House, whose management enlarged the hotel twice but never yielded to the modern decadent fondness for private bathrooms. The Rodick, which a decade earlier was one of the best-known society hotels in America, was to linger on for another twelve years before expiring in 1906.

The decade of the 1880s saw more cottages built than any other period in Bar Harbor history, and they were no longer simple. They included Mrs.

George Bowler's (and later Joseph Pulitzer's) Chatwold, James G. Blaine's Stanwood, and John A. Morris's Bogue Chitto. Within a few years, there were some 175 cottages in Bar Harbor, occupied during the summer by their owners, the elite of New York, Boston, Philadelphia, Washington, Chicago (in that order), and lesser cities. Clubs were organized to cater to them. The earliest was the Oasis Club, an exclusively male preserve. As its name implies, it offered a refuge to civilized men from the tyranny of Maine's prohibition law. The Oasis later moved to more imposing surroundings and became the Mount Desert Reading Room. For the athletic, there was the Mount Desert Canoe Club, whose stated object was "to develop and perpetuate birch-bark canoeing." Early photographs of Frenchman Bay show a flotilla of canoes, and there were usually one or two canoes drawn up on the beach at one of the Porcupines.

Most of the summer society were members of the Kebo Valley Club, which opened in 1889. The building contained a theatre and a restaurant; the grounds included a race track, a baseball field, several tennis and croquet lawns, and, most important, from 1892 on, a golf course. Visiting dignitaries were usually entertained at Kebo.

There were dances at the hotels every night during August, receptions and dinners at the cottages, parties on board the yachts, picnics, sailing parties, garden parties, and concerts, and always good conversation — the best, according to Barrett Wendell of Harvard, to be found anywhere in America.

IN THE EARLY DAYS OF BAR HARBOR.

The natural attractions of Mount Desert brought the best and brightest talkers to the island, and a steady stream of journalists came to describe its beauties for the folks back home. Since Europe was still the fount of culture, it was characteristic of that time, as a character in Charles Dudley Warner's *Their Pilgrimage* observed, "to stick a foreign name on everything." "Mt. Desert is not pure Norway," wrote a chronicler in *Century Magazine*. "It is Norway and Italy combined." According to the scribe, it was worth months of waiting to stand on the summit of Sargent Mountain "breathing in the ozone of Scandinavia and feasting my eyes on a vision filled with the dreamy poetry of the South."

The road along the Bluffs was called the Cornice Road after its supposed resemblance to the *Corniche*, which follows the rocky Italian coast between Sorrento and Salerno. Wanderers on "Tyrolean footpaths" saw darkly silhouetted against the sunset glow a pile akin to "some hoary Romanesque castle on guard above the Rhine," while beneath the tree-trunks "one spies over the streamlet a jut of red crag, a sheet of blue-gray ocean, and a distant peak that one feels *must* be Fujiyama." For the literary-minded, the south ridge of Green Mountain brought back "the atmosphere of the Lake Country of Wordsworth," and even the Bar Harbor Swimming Club recalled "Smollett's word-pictures of Bath," an evocation exceedingly difficult to credit on the basis of surviving photographs. (One authentic foreign note was the presence in the summers during the 1890s of the British, Turkish, and Austrian embassies, who were there to escape the heat of Washington.)

The years just prior to World War I have been called the Confident Years and the Age of Innocence. They have been described in memoirs bathed in a sort of twilight mist — a portrait of a society that seems as remote to us today as Regency England.

It was a world of ease and well-being for the very small minority whose houses and playgrounds appear on the pages that follow. The stability of the era may be illustrated by the fact that when George M. McFadden bought George Vanderbilt's Pointe d'Acadie shortly after the end of World War I, it was the first large piece of Bar Harbor property to change hands in fifteen years. In the next three years, forty-seven cottages would change hands.

The founding of Lafayette (later Acadia) National Park in 1919 and the introduction of the automobile made the island accessible to hundreds of thousands of tourists who would transform the island — or at least the one-third of it that lies outside the park — into something beyond the wildest imaginings of Tobias Roberts or, for that matter, Weir Mitchell, who never wanted cars on the island in the first place.

It is popularly believed that the Great Fire of 1947 finished off Bar Harbor as a resort. But the fire was for many a blessing in disguise. Although a third of the 222 cottages burned, many were already empty or for sale. Bar Harbor had tottered through the depression and World War II, and the 1947 Cottage Directory reveals that only 135 cottages were occupied that summer. By this time, Bar Harbor was already "lost," although a few relics of happier days were to linger on, rather like the heath hens on Martha's Vineyard.

Another casualty of that memorable year was the Pennsylvania Railroad's "Bar Harbor Express" from Philadelphia. The steamboat *J. T. Morse* of fond memory had made her last run from Rockland on September 21, 1931; the Portland steamers were by that time long gone.

A FORMAL CALL.

It is not within the scope of this book to comment on the present era of mass tourism. Main Street in August cries out for a Swift to portray it, but the hills and woodland trails, the ocean, the streams and ponds, and the invigorating air have remained inviolate. (Perhaps we should be thankful for the timidity of the many tourists who do not wander far from the road.)

In October of 1884, the Mount Desert *Herald* reported the elder's prayer, "Oh, Lord, now that our summer visitors have departed, wilt Thou take their places in our hearts." The attitude of the natives toward the newcomers remains substantially the same — a mixture of avarice and amusement that is always tempered with courtesy.

Although many of the buildings illustrated in this book are of architectural and historical significance, and their loss destroyed a tangible link with a gaudy past, this is not the forum for arguing the case for historic preservation. What follows is simply a pictorial record of many, but by no means all of the homes that have vanished, together with brief sketches of their principal inmates.

BAR HARBOR SEEN FROM BAR ISLAND (CIRCA 1890)

The Cottages

Birch Point

The distinction of being Bar Harbor's first cottager belongs to Alpheus Hardy, a wealthy and cultured clipper trade merchant from Boston and a leader in every religious and philanthropic movement in that city. The story of how he came to Bar Harbor sounds apocryphal.

It seems that one day in the early 1860s an elderly lady came into his downtown Boston office selling medicinal and culinary herbs. Hardy chatted with her and was enchanted by her description of the mountains, woodland paths, and rocky shores of the island where she had grown them. Hardy determined to visit the island.

In the spring of 1865, with his two sons returned from the Civil War and in need of a rest, the family set out by steamer for Bucksport, traveling the rest of the way by horse and carriage. He came, saw, and was conquered. He purchased a piece of land on Birch Point from "Uncle" Stephen Higgins for $300, and in 1868 built the first cottage on the point not far from the present location of the Bar Harbor Motor Inn swimming pool.

Hardy persuaded many of his Boston friends to spend the summer in Bar Harbor, including his business partner, Charles J. Morrill, who built Redwood in 1879, and his former ward, J. Montgomery Sears, who built The Briars in 1881. Hardy died in 1887 from complications from an accident in which a pair of scissors fell on his foot. His widow continued to spend the summers at Ullikana, a new cottage they had built in the Field in 1885. She died there in 1904.

Birch Point was demolished in 1938.

Minot Cottage

In 1869 George Richards Minot and F. M. Weld of Boston bought 2 2/3 acres of land in the Field for $2,500. The Messrs. Hamor built houses for the pair — each house was two stories, each measured fifty-three by forty-two feet. Minot's three daughters — Bessie, Mary, and Louisa — were members of Weir Mitchell's set and were lifelong spinsters. Louisa summered in Bar Harbor for more than sixty years, until her death in 1932. We are indebted to Cleveland Amory for the information that Louisa had red hair and rattling dentures.

The Minot Cottage was torn down in 1939.

Pointe d'Acadie

The first New Yorker to build in Bar Harbor was Gouverneur Morris Ogden, who died on the island in 1884.* Originally called Watersmeet, the house was designed by the noted New York architect Charles Coolidge Haight (1841–1917). It was built in 1868–69.

The fastidious and romantic George Washington Vanderbilt II purchased Ogden Point in 1889 for $200,000, changed the name of the cottage to Pointe d'Acadie, and remodeled it. He installed Bar Harbor's first private swimming pool. He almost drowned in it one day but was rescued by a young woman. Vanderbilt, who inherited $20 million from his father, rewarded her with a gift of sweet peas.

The house was later owned by Philadelphia cotton broker George H. McFadden. It was torn down in 1956.

*In time, New Yorkers came to dominate the Bar Harbor summer colony. The 1916 cottage directory lists 217 cottagers, of whom 115 were from New York. Next in numbers of cottagers are Boston (28), Philadelphia (23), and Washington (12). Most of the rest came from remote outposts in the hinterland (e.g., Chicago).

Ledge Lawn

Mary Shannon of Newton, Massachusetts, first visited Bar Harbor in 1865 for a two-week vacation. In 1871 she returned for the summer and never missed a summer after that until she died in 1901. In 1876 she purchased seventy acres of land and built the Shingle-Style cottage Ledge Lawn on Mount Desert Street. The architect was probably W. Jordan, the contractor. Miss Shannon donated a strip of land to widen Ledgelawn Avenue and two parcels of land which became the present Glen Mary Park for children. She also presented the town with the first flags that were flown over schoolhouses in the area. However, her offer of a 1,600-square-foot lot for a town hall — on condition it cost at least ten thousand dollars and that she select the architect — was voted down at the spring Town Meeting.

Ledge Lawn was demolished in 1902, and a new cottage was built on the site in 1904.

Schooner Head

Built in 1876 by George Hale, this was the summer home for many years of Richard Walden Hale, Massachusetts lawyer, member of the House of Representatives, and a U. S. Commissioner for eighteen years. A champion of free speech and public expression, he was a vice-president of the Ford Hall Forum and active in its affairs. He was author of *The Dreyfus Case*, and *The Letters of Warwick Green*. His son, Richard W. Hale, Jr., was the author of *The Story of Bar Harbor*.

The house burned in the 1947 fire.

The Craigs and The Eyrie

THE CRAIGS

Appropriately named, The Craigs* and The Eyrie stood on top of the hill above the present Spring Street and Glen Mary Park.

The Craigs, 1879–80, was designed by the remarkable Bruce Price, who made an indelible mark on the hotel and cottage architecture of the period. Although built as a "cottage," it was described by architectural historian Vincent Scully as "a kind of fantastic feudal castle, a hodge-podge of picturesque bits and romantic skylines, an exacerbation of the industrialist's dream of the picturesque."

The Craigs was built for Dr. Robert Amory, Professor of Physiology at Bowdoin Medical School. He practiced medicine during the summer at Bar Harbor from 1880 to 1887,

---

*Craig is a Scottish and North of England variant of *crag*.

THE EYRIE

when he retired. The cottage was
later occupied by the James Amorys.
It was demolished in 1946.

The Eyrie was designed by
the equally renowned William Ralph
Emerson of Boston. Erected in 1881,
it was owned by Dr. Amory and then
by his daughter, Mrs. Augustus Thorndike. It burned in September 1887,
was rebuilt in 1900, and finally was
demolished in 1942. A new cottage
was built on the site in 1951 by Mr.
and Mrs. R. Amory Thorndike. Mrs.
Thorndike lives there still.

Bruce Price

Bruce Price, who was born in Cumberland, Maryland, in 1845, studied architecture in Baltimore and abroad. After practicing in Baltimore and Wilkes-Barre, Pennsylvania, he moved to New York. In addition to The Craigs, his most notable work in Bar Harbor was the West End Hotel, 1878–79. His Bar Harbor cottage designs included Casa Far Niente, Villa Mary, the Lombard Cottage, the Turrets (1893–95), Witchcliff, and others. Other works were the Roosevelt cottage at Oyster Bay, New York, the American Surety and St. James buildings in New York, Hotchkiss Preparatory School at Lakeville, Connecticut, Chateau Frontenac, Quebec, the railroad stations at Windsor Street and East End and the Royal Victoria Academy in Montreal, and the Welch Dormitory at Yale. The high point of his career, says Vincent Scully, was the series of cottages he began to build in 1885 for Pierre Lorillard's residential development at Tuxedo Park, New York. This "elegant gentleman and erratic genius" (Scully) was also the father of Mrs. Emily Post, who made a career out of good manners. Price died in 1903.

William Ralph Emerson

Born in 1833, Emerson began to practice architecture in the 1870s. His Redwood, built in 1879 for C. J. Morrill, has been called the first fully developed example of "Shingle Style." Over the next six years, his work dominated all others in Bar Harbor and was a source of inspiration to those who followed. In addition to The Eyrie, his achievements included the following "lost" cottages: The Briars, Brook End, Bournemouth, Edgemere, Highbrook, Homewood, Mossley Hall (which Scully called Emerson's best house), Shore Acres, Thirlstane, and the totally shingled Church of St. Sylvia. His disciples, Portland's John Calvin Stevens and Albert Winslow Cobb, wrote of him:

Now this man's work is lovely because there is instilled into it the power of a chivalrous, joyous nature, revering everything pure and holy in his fellow-creatures; while scorning everything that is extravagant, meretricious. The virtue which another of his line instils through his philosophy [Ralph Waldo Emerson was a distant relation], *he himself instils in American life through his Art.*

Emerson died in 1917.

Old Farm

This cottage, by Alexander F. Oakey of New York, stood on a broad, flat cliff at Compass Harbor. It was built in 1876–77 for Charles F. Dorr of Boston, father of George Bucknam Dorr, a lifelong bachelor and scholar who devoted not only his life but also much of his personal wealth to the establishment of Lafayette (Acadia) National Park. Sixty years later, George Dorr recalled:

"It was the first house in Bar Harbor to be really well built; and well built it was with nothing spared in work or material. The first story we built of granite split out from tumbled boulders in the gorge, weathered and warm-toned . . . and at the last some brick was used that added their touch of color to the warm-toned granite. Above that first story, all was shingled with shingles of the warm brown, never rotting California redwood.

"In the interior, the frame was built with extra strength — my father saw to that — while all the interior finish was skillfully and carefully worked out from the best of Michigan white pine, Maine wood of similar grain being no longer obtainable. The floors throughout were of well-seasoned native oak, birch and maple, and better one could not have. The carpenters and the Maine folk have a genius for that work, took great pridce in their work and endless time about it."

The Dorrs were fond of entertaining, and Old Farm welcomed a steady stream of eminent worthies. The guest book survives and bears the signatures of Chester Arthur, Julia Ward Howe, Barrett Wendell, Weir Mitchell, Josiah Royce, E. L. Godkin, William James, and Oliver Wendell Holmes the elder. When Holmes, a frequent visitor, was seventy-nine years old, he was seized by the divine afflatus:

La Maison d'Or

*From this fair house behold on either
   side
The restful mountains or the restless
   sea,
So the warm sheltering walls of life
   divide
Time and its tides from still eternity.*

*Look on the waves; their stormy
   voices teach
That not on earth may toil and
   struggle cease.
Look on the mountains; better far
   than speech
Their silent promise of eternal peace.*

George Dorr was a tall, gaunt man with a walrus mustache. He read Homer in the original, swam winter (!) and summer off the beach at Cromwell Harbor, and tramped endlessly over the hills and forests of his beloved island. Nearly blind, he spent the last years of his life in the caretaker's cottage on the estate and died in 1944 at the age of ninety. Old Farm was torn down in 1951.

The Lombard Cottage, Witchcliff, and Villa Mary

Built on Eden Street in 1880 for Edith Lombard and Mrs. A. F. Manning, the Lombard Cottage and Witchcliff (both by Bruce Price) were demolished in 1927 and 1936, respectively. Villa Mary still stands. Witchcliff was rebuilt as a modern cottage.

Brook End

This cottage, by William Ralph Emerson, stood at the outlet of Duck Brook. It was built in 1880–81 for General W. F. Smith, an outspoken and controversial figure during the Civil War. After the disaster at Fredericksburg, he wrote an intemperate letter to President Lincoln. Later he criticized (justifiably) General Meade to President Grant. After the war, he became police commissioner of New York.

In 1889 the cottage was purchased by Dr. Robert Abbe of New York, a distinguished surgeon. Dr. Abbe pioneered various cranial, esophageal, and intestinal operations, worked with Madame Curie in Paris, and was one of the first to employ radium in clinical practice.

In 1922 Dr. Abbe was attracted by a local shop-window display of Indian artifacts dug from shell heaps near Gouldsboro. From then on, Dr. Abbe immersed himself in the study of archaeology. As his private collection grew, augmented by the collections of his friends, the need for a building to house them became evident. Funds were raised to build the Robert Abbe Museum at Sieur de Monts, which was dedicated in August 1928, just a few months after Dr. Abbe's death. The relief maps that adorn the walls of the museum are the work of this talented man.

Dr. Abbe also worked closely with President Charles Eliot of Harvard and with George Bucknam Dorr toward the creation of Lafayette (Acadia) National Park. He has been called the best-loved summer resident of Bar Harbor.

Brook End was demolished about 1963.

The Briars

Designed by William Ralph Emerson, this cottage was built in 1881 for J. Montgomery Sears of Boston. It stood on the Shore Path, at the end of Wayman Lane. Sears, and later his son, was invariably described in newspapers of the day as "Boston's largest taxpayer." By 1908 the automobile had replaced the guillotine as a method for dispatching the aristocracy, and the younger Sears was thrown from his roadster and killed instantly. That summer the house was rented by John D. Rockefeller Jr., whose son Nelson was born there.

In 1909, young Edward Beale McLean and his bride, the former Evalyn Walsh, "took a fancy to the place," as she wrote later, and her father bought it for them. Tom Walsh was an immigrant Irish carpenter who, after twenty years of toil in Colorado, had struck it rich in the fabulous Camp Bird gold mine. He then moved to Washington, built a sixty-room *Stadtpalast*, and became the friend of such notables as President McKinley and King Leopold of the Belgians. His son-in-law, Ned, was the spoiled and dimwitted son of John Roll McLean, the corrupt and politically ambitious owner of the Cincinnati *Enquirer* and the Washington *Post*.

It was inevitable that Ned and Evalyn would meet in the whirl of Washington society. They were engaged a half-dozen times before they finally eloped in the summer of 1908, embarking for Europe with a joint budget of $200,000 and, as Evalyn's friend Lucius Beebe wrote, "parental assurances that when this was gone, there was more where it had come from." As it turned out, they did need more — much more.

Ned's chief interests in life were alcohol and fast cars. When John McLean died in 1916, Ned became editor and publisher of the *Post*, a friend of the Warren Hardings, and a charter member of the president's so-called kitchen cabinet of poker-playing cronies whom he served in the capacity of resident buffoon. He is remembered today chiefly for his humiliating appearance before the congressional committee investigating the Teapot Dome scandal. The affable Ned, always ready to oblige a friend, committed perjury to protect Albert Fall. Within a few years he was confined to a private mental hospital in Maryland, where he died in 1941. At the time of his death, he was insisting to all outsiders that he was *not* Ned McLean.

Evalyn was nearly as fond of the bottle as Ned, but probably was more intelligent. Her weakness was jewelry. Whenever her soul languished and her mind filled with thoughts of doom, she would make a beeline for Cartier's. Buying jewelry, she explained, was therapeutic.

On one of their frequent trips to Paris, Evalyn purchased the Hope Diamond. Although she had it exorcised by a priest, she would not escape the myth of its baleful influence.

Her son Vinson, whom the tabloids dubbed "the hundred-million-dollar baby," was killed by an automobile, and her daughter committed suicide shortly before Evalyn's own death in 1947.

The Briars was torn down in 1968, except for a sevants' wing, which was made into a guest house.

"When President Taft came to Bar Harbor on the Mayflower, *I was working as a salesman at the Mount Desert Nursery store on Main Street. Evalyn Walsh McLean came into the store about eleven one morning before his arrival and said to me that he was coming and she would like to decorate the saloon on the* Mayflower *and what would I suggest? I went to the ice box and said that I thought that American Beauty roses would look nice. She asked the price. I told her the twelve-inch were $12 a dozen, the eighteen-inch $18 a dozen. She said, "I will have one hundred dozen of the eighteen-inch ones."*

— Chester Wescott

Edgemere

Another of William Ralph Emerson's houses, Edgemere was built on the Shore Path in 1881 for Thomas Musgrave. Other owners were William Sherman, Chester Barnett, and Beatrix Farrand (*see* Reef Point). It was torn down in 1938.

Guy's Cliff

This Eden Street cottage was built for Charles T. How, who, after having long lived abroad, arrived in Bar Harbor in the summer of 1870 and was so charmed with the beauty of the place that he made it his summer home. The following year he bought an enormous tract known as the Woodbury Farm (roughly west of Cleftstone Road), and in time became probably the largest landowner in Bar Harbor. How spent $125,000 opening new roads in the village. His most notable gift was the (today) curiously neglected Fawn Pond, which he presented to the Village Improvement Association.

The original architect of Guy's Cliff was W. Jordan, but the building was remodeled by Guy Lowell's office when James Byrne bought it from J. J. O'Brien in 1926. The previous owner was Edwin C. Cushman, a Newport, Rhode Island, lawyer, who named the cottage for his oldest son.

James Byrne (1857–1942) was a New York corporation lawyer and leading Catholic layman. Indeed, he was the first Roman Catholic to be elected to the Harvard Corporation. He had strong sympathies for the downtrodden, and thus was a leading advocate of higher education for women. He was also actively interested in Negro education. One of his daughters became Mrs. Hamilton Fish Armstrong, another Mrs. Walter Lippmann. Byrne willed the cottage to the Oblate Fathers for their seminary.

The building was subsequently purchased by Bernard Cough and leased to the College of the Atlantic, which later bought it. It stands today somewhat altered from the picture above.

Highbrook

Still another of William Ralph Emerson's cottages, Highbrook was built in 1881. Its first owner was Mary (Mrs. James) Leeds of Boston. From 1925 it was owned by Mrs. A. M. Patterson, daughter of Mrs. J. Madison Taylor of Philadelphia, a painter of miniatures who summered in Bar Harbor for three-quarters of a century. The cottage, which stood on Highbrook Road, burned in 1947.

Meadowridge

Meadowridge was built by Albert Higgins (after whom Albert Meadow is named) in 1881. It was purchased in 1885 by Parke Godwin (1816–1904), the last survivor of that small group of editors who gave character and individuality to the New York newspaper world of the 1840s and 1850s. The intimate friend and son-in-law of William Cullen Bryant, Godwin was a contemporary and friend of Horace Greeley, Henry Raymond, George William Curtis, Charles A. Dana, and other journalistic giants of the period. Godwin was interested in the voluntary associa-

tion ideas that took hold in New England about 1840 and culminated in the communistic Brook Farm community, whose newspaper he edited. He was famous as a speaker and essayist and wrote criticism on Emerson, de Tocqueville, Thackeray, and Shakespeare. In later years, the cheerful, white-maned, venerable Godwin was a familiar figure on the streets of Bar Harbor. He was said to be the last of the summer contingent to leave in the fall.

The house was then owned by Fred Jellison, and later by Alice Kiaer, and was demolished about 1955.

Shore Acres

This large estate, by William Ralph Emerson, was built in 1881 for Dr. Haskett Derby of Boston, who first visited Bar Harbor in 1869, and built his first cottage the next year. Dr. Derby was a descendant of Elias Haskett Derby, noted Salem, Massachusetts, merchant and shipbuilder, and the richest man in America in the 18th century.

Dr. Derby died in 1914. Later the cottage was occupied by Mrs. Haskett Derby until 1936. Shore Acres stood on the Shore Path, adjacent to Albert Meadow, until it was demolished about 1957.

Thirlstane

Mrs. Rebecca Scott of Washington, D.C., had this Emerson-designed house built in 1881. After Mrs. Scott's death, Colonel (later General) Edward Morrell of Philadelphia bought the house in 1897. He had occupied the house for the previous two summers. Colonel Morrell made many alterations and improvements, including a new veranda and an addition to house a library. Morrell was an enthusiastic horseman and the owner of Robin Hood Park at the foot of Newport (now Champlain) Mountain. When the Horse Show and Fair Association was founded in 1900, he made the park available to them. After Colonel Morrell's death, his widow presented the park to the people of Bar Harbor. The grounds are now part of the Jackson Laboratory.

In 1926, William Pierson Hamilton, son-in-law of the elder J. P. Morgan and great-grandson of Alexander Hamilton, bought Thirlstane and added a swimming pool. He began to develop model farms in the area and purchased several in Salisbury Cove, along the Shore Road, and in Lamoine and Trenton — nine farms in all, totaling fifteen hundred acres and employing 100 people. He bred sheep and raised hogs, poultry, and cattle. In 1939 he sold all the livestock and most of the farms. He gave the Salisbury Cove farm to the Jackson Laboratory, which established the laboratory now called Hamilton Station.

One summer Hamilton published his own newspaper — The Mount Desert *Herald* — at a cost of one million dollars, because he was unhappy with the local papers' coverage of his dinner parties.

Thirlstane burned in the 1947 fire. One may wander about the ruins today on the top of Hamilton Hill.

Casa Far Niente

In 1892 Bar Harbor gained one of its most illustrious summer residents when S. Weir Mitchell, bored with Newport, quit the Rhode Island resort and moved into the West Street cottage shown here.

Mitchell was a Philadelphia neurologist and author whose novels — particularly *Hugh Wynne, Free Quaker* — were popular in their day. A connoisseur of wine, he contributed *A Madeira Party* to American letters. He also wrote poetry, much of it at Bar Harbor on such subjects as Cadillac Cliffs, Sargent Mountain, and — a favorite of his — Fawn Pond. His first scientific work dealt with snake venom, but he became best known for his rest cure for nervous exhaustion. The latter involved the systematic use of massage, until then an esoteric practice virtually unheard of outside the Orient. (If Mitchell was indeed the first to employ massage in the West, it dwarfs all of his other accomplishments!) This gifted man is also said to have advised Edith Wharton to write, and fellow Philadelphian Owen Wister to go west.

It was Mitchell's custom to leave Philadelphia about the first of June and return in November. After a few weeks of salmon fishing in Canada, Mitchell would descend on Casa Far Niente. His diary entry for July 29, 1901, reads: "Bar Harbor. In my house at five. Oh, Lord, I am glad!"

One of the best of the walkers and talkers, Mitchell's "lean, active, knickerbockered shape" was a familiar sight along the trails. His conversational circle included all of the prominent bluestockings, scholarly divines, and eminent pedagogues such as Charles William Eliot, Seth Low, and Daniel Coit Gilman. He died in 1914.

Casa Far Niente, which was designed by Bruce Price and built for William Rice in 1882, was demolished in 1943.

Rocklyn

ROCKLYN COTTAGE, BAR HARBOR.

Rocklyn was built in 1881–82 for James Hinch. Among its subsequent owners were "Commodore" Philip Livingston of New York, and the Bar Harbor Canoe Club. Livingston, an impeccable figure in tails, and prominent at horse shows and other social events, apparently fell on evil days, for he turned up during the Depression as a floorwalker at Macy's.

Like its neighbors on Eden Street, Rocklyn burned in 1947.

Chatwold

The most extraordinary cottager in Bar Harbor's history was the publisher Joseph Pulitzer, whose egalitarian New York *World* regularly assailed the "vulgar wealthy."

When Pulitzer leased Chatwold from Louise Bowler Livingston in June 1893, he was rapidly going blind and suffering from asthma, insomnia, nervous exhaustion, and fits of depression alternating with periods of incredible bursts of energy and euphoria (manic-depressive psychosis?). He purchased Chatwold the following year and immediately set about making extensive additions and renovations, including the $100,000 granite structure (shown on the far right in the photo) waggishly named the "Tower of Silence" by its inmates. It was painstakingly designed to keep out noise but did not do so. Behind the Tower of Silence was a little balcony overhanging Bear Brook. Here Pulitzer achieved tranquility.

Pulitzer loved luxury and spent at least twelve hours of the day in bed. When he stayed at hotels, rooms had to be kept vacant above, below, and on either side of him. The foghorn at the Egg Rock lighthouse drove him frantic, and in vain he importuned the government to have it silenced. He believed in liberty and equality, but not fraternity, and held himself aloof. He rarely visited New York; he ran his newspapers from Bar Harbor (where he spent the summer and fall), Jekyll Island, Georgia (winter), and Europe. The bill for maintaining these residencies totaled about $350,000 a year. His yacht *Liberty* was always in commission; her operating costs, with repairs, ran close to $200,000 a year. "Find a breeze," was the most frequent sailing order from the asthmatic sybarite.

He loved horses: the stables at Chatwold held twenty-six animals. Pulitzer also enjoyed swimming, and built Bar Harbor's first *heated* swimming pool (Vanderbilt's pool at Pointe d'Acadie was fed from the ocean). Among his other gifts, he was a virtuoso in the use of profanity, and he is credited with inventing the American custom of inserting *goddam* into other words to give them greater forensic emphasis (e.g., "inde*goddam*pendent").

His closest friends at Bar Harbor were S. Weir Mitchell and the J. Madison Taylors, the three college presidents Charles Eliot, Seth Low, and Daniel Gilman, and the Austro-Hungarian minister Baron Hengelmuller.

Pulitzer died in 1911; the *World* ended in 1931; Chatwold, which stood on Schooner Head Road, was demolished in 1945.

Clovercroft

This Eden Street cottage, by
Rotch & Tilden of Boston, was built
in 1883–84 for George Place of New
York and his wife, the former Iphy-
nia G. Livor. It burned in 1947.

Homewood

The work of William Ralph Emerson, Homewood stood on Eagle Lake Road from 1883 to October 1947. Among its owners were Mrs. M. D. Sanders and Hugh Scott, both Philadelphians. As Cleveland Amory points out, Bar Harbor was renowned not only for walkers and talkers: the Misses Helen Sanders and Marie Scott were famous local belles.

Mossley Hall

Perhaps William Ralph Emerson's best house, Mossley Hall was called by Vincent Scully "a 19th-century romantic landscape painter's ideal of an upland dwelling, perched lightly above misty valleys, its rough texture and warm colors in harmony with the colors and textures of its terrain."

Sited on the wooded hill on Norman Road, Mossley Hall was built in 1882–83 for William B. Howard of Chicago, who is reputed to have laid more miles of railroad than any man in the country, including the Nickel Plate Railroad. He also built the Indiana State House and was identified with construction of the New York Aqueduct. The house was torn down about 1945.

Mizzentop

Designed by H. L. Putnam of Boston, this Cleftstone Road cottage was built in 1883–84 for Mrs. William Morris Hunt, widow of the artist. Her daughters, eccentric and Junoesque, married the Horatio Slaters, father and son. Enid, the older, married the son; Bey, the younger, married Horatio Slater, Sr.

The next owner of Mizzentop was Robert Hall McCormick (1847–1917), grandson of the inventor of the reaping machine, who retired from the family firm in 1889 to invest successfully in downtown Chicago real estate. McCormick's chief interests were horses, yachting, and art. He owned Gainsboroughs, Reynoldses, and Turners, and became director of the Art Institute of Chicago.

Finally, Mizzentop was owned by Henry Morgenthau, lawyer, financier, and diplomat (U. S. Ambassador to Turkey), and father of Franklin Delano Roosevelt's Secretary of the Treasury.

The house burned in 1947.

Fred C. Lyman and Co., Real Estate Agents, described "Mizzentop" in a mid-1940s brochure:

"Mizzentop" is located in the Cleftstone area of Bar Harbor, Maine, overlooking Frenchman's Bay, the Porcupine Islands, and the Gouldsboro Hills in the distance.

The main residence is flanked . . . by a formal garden with a granite pillared pergola, and . . . by the rose garden and fountain.

Maine granite predominates; *the first story of the main house is granite, likewise the pergola, and granite walls separate the elevations wherever lawns and gardens are terraced.*

The dwelling is substantially built, hardwood floors throughout, plastered or panelled and thoroughly furnished. Three master bedrooms, each with a fireplace and bath, and two of these rooms opening on the large porch overlooking the bay. Five guests' rooms and two baths on the third floor.

The large living room is panelled, fireplace; large reception hall, fireplace; powder room, lavatory, coat room, large open porch. Four maids' rooms in main house and six rooms and bath in adjacent laundry building.

Taxes $1,281.32 Price $40,000

Reef Point

This Shore Path cottage, by Rotch & Tilden, was built in 1883 for Mrs. Cadwalader Jones. Born Mary Cadwalader Rawle in Philadelphia, she married and divorced Frederick R. Jones, brother of Edith Wharton, with whom she remained a close friend and literary agent. Mrs. Jones was co-founder of the Bar Harbor Ladies Club in 1897. A woman of intellect and humor, she lived in New York's Greenwich Village and numbered among her intimate friends Henry James, Henry and Brooks Adams, Marion Crawford, and Theodore Roosevelt. She died in London in 1935. Edith Wharton, her benefactress for many years, rushed over to London to handle the funeral arrangements. Mrs. Jones was buried in Hertfordshire next to Mrs. Humphrey Davy.

Mrs. Jones's daughter, Beatrix Farrand, was a landscape gardener of great distinction. Described as a perfectionist and a demanding woman to work for, she is best remembered by the profession for her garden at Dumbarton Oaks in Washington, D.C., her work in planting design at Princeton and Yale, and her participation in founding the American Society of Landscape Architects. She refused to call herself an "architect," adding "landscape gardener" to her signature on plans and drawings.

It is likely that her aunt Edith Wharton, an amateur architecture historian, had great influence on her choice of career. Her family's social standing provided a steady supply of wealthy and famous clients, including her mother's friend TR, John D. Rockefeller, Jr., J. P. Morgan, and Mrs. Woodrow Wilson. At age forty-two, she married Max Farrand, Professor of History at Yale and later Director of the Huntington Library in Pasadena, California. The Farrands always spent their summers at Reef Point.

After Max Farrand's death in 1945, Mrs. Farrand dedicated herself to the development and management of Reef Point, which she had established in 1939 as a botanical garden and reference library for public use. The project was abandoned in 1955, however, in part due to the lack of students of landscape design in the vicinity, and in part because she felt it her duty to make the material available as part of a teaching institution where it would be used as part of the curriculum. The library and related collections were given to the University of California at Berkeley. The gardens were discontinued, and Mrs. Farrand disposed of the acreage and her old home.

Mrs. Farrand was the landscape architect for many summer estates on the island, including Edgar Scott's Chiltern, Dr. Robert Abbe's Brook End, Mrs. Robert McCormick's Bournemouth, the Stotesburys' Wingwood, and the Rockefeller Gardens at Seal Harbor.

Mrs. Farrand died in 1959 and was buried in Bar Harbor. Reef Point was torn down in 1955.

Bournemouth

By 1885–86, when Bournemouth was built, Eden Street from Duck Brook to Hulls Cove was well on its way to becoming an uninterrupted row of cottages. This William Ralph Emerson house was built for W. B. Walley, a Boston lawyer, and was later occupied by Mrs. Archibald Cary Harrison,* daughter-in-law of Constance Cary Harrison, and from 1925 by Mrs. Robert Hall McCormick, Jr.

Bournemouth escaped the 1947 fire to survive until 1979.

---

*Archibald Cary Harrison was one of three sons of Burton Harrison and Constance Cary Harrison. Mrs. Harrison wrote several novels dealing with New York society and Virginia life, and an autobiography, *Recollections Grave and Gay*. She occupied a cottage (still standing) called Sea Urchins. Another son, Francis Burton Harrison, was the owner of Greenway Court.

Devilstone

This Shore Path cottage, the work of Rotch & Tilden of Boston, was built in 1885 for Mrs. George Bowler. Subsequent owners were New York banker James T. Woodward, Mrs. Thomas Scott, Clement Newbold (one of the last ten members of the Bar Harbor Reading Room, but that is another story, p. 116), and Miss Frances Colman, who changed the name to Eaglestone. (When I inquired as to the reason for the name change, I was told that if I knew Miss Colman I would not need to ask.) The main section of the house was torn down in 1968; remaining are a wing added on in 1928 and a library made into a small cottage.

Stanwood

Designed by W. M. Camac of Philadelphia, Stanwood was built in 1885–86 for James G. Blaine. Blaine — the "Plumed Knight" or the "Continental Liar from the State of Maine," depending upon your point of view — was born in West Brownsville, Pennsylvania. He did not settle in Maine, the state with which he is identified, until 1854, when he became editor of Augusta's Kennebec *Journal*; later he was editor of the Portland *Advertiser*. He became a state legislator in 1858. Four years later he was elected to the United States Congress. He was Speaker of the House, a Senator, and twice Secretary of State. In 1876 and 1880 he was a willing but unwanted candidate for the Republican presidential nomination, which he finally captured in 1884, only to lose narrowly to Grover Cleveland after a bitter and rancorous campaign. By all accounts, Blaine was a man of great personal magnetism, wit, and charm. He died in 1893.

Blaine's daughter Margaret married Walter Damrosch, the composer and conductor. Damrosch was a pioneer in concerts for children and radio broadcasting. His programs for young people on NBC every Friday morning and the words, "Good morning, my dear children," were familiar to a generation of Americans. Damrosch's enthusiasms did not go beyond European classical and 19th-century music. When Leopold Stokowski proposed broadcasting modern music into school classrooms, Damrosch protested that to perform such "experiments on helpless children is criminal." He died in 1950 and is buried in Bar Harbor. One of Damrosch's sons-in-law, Thomas K. Finletter, became a lifelong summer resident of Bar Harbor.

Stanwood stood on Norman Road until the fire of October 1947.

Dust Pan Cottage

This interestingly named cottage, built on Eden Street in 1886, was designed by Boston's Rotch & Tilden for Rufus King, Cincinnati lawyer and philanthropist. It was later owned by Mrs. W. E. Montgomery and James Cunningham. It burned in 1947.

Fabian Cottage

The John Clark cottage shown here was built on Eden Street for R. L. Fabian in 1885–86. A tower was added the following year, and a two-story addition in 1889. The cottage was torn down in 1975.

Italian Villa

This Eden Street House by Rotch & Tilden was built in 1886. It was the home of Dr. George Harris, a native of East Machais, Maine. Dr. Harris was a graduate of Amherst College and Andover Theological Seminary and was ordained a Congregational minister. After serving in Providence and teaching at Andover, he became president of Amherst from 1899 to 1912. His religious works include *Moral Evolution* and *A Century's Change in Religion*. His son George was a well-known tenor who performed at Bar Harbor's Building of Arts.

The cottage, which was subsequently owned by F. McCormick-Goodhart of Washington, D.C., and Hobe Sound, Florida, was destroyed by fire in 1947.

Blair Eyrie

One of Bar Harbor's largest cottages, Blair Eyrie on Highbrook Road was originally called Avamaya. It was built in 1888 by Sidney V. Stratton of Frank Quinby Associates for Major George Wheeler, U.S. Corps of Engineers. It was purchased in 1901 by DeWitt C. Blair of the New York banking firm. When Blair died in 1915, the subhead in the Bar Harbor *Record* proclaimed: "Notable Summer Resident — He Gave His Sons, C. Ledyard and John I., Each $7,000,000 Last Christmas." Blair Eyrie was demolished about 1935, and a nursing facility was built on the site in 1976.

Bogue Chitto

According to Richard Hale, this Hulls Cove house, designed by W. H. Day, "evoked a burst of applause in the Mount Desert *Herald*" upon its completion in 1888. It was built for John A. Morris, the "Louisiana Lottery King." His son, Dave Hennen Morris, was a lawyer, homeopathic physician, an accomplished violinist, yachtsman, tennis player, president of the Automobile Club of America, and a business and educational leader. In his spare time, he operated one of America's most prominent racing stables. A close friend of Franklin Roosevelt, he became Ambassador to Belgium and Minister to Luxembourg in the 1930s. Bogue Chitto, which is derived from the Louisiana Indian dialect meaning "Brook of Shadows," was demolished about 1961.

Talleyrand

Along with Charles T. How, his real estate associate, DeGrasse Fox of Philadelphia was an active land developer who did much to "improve" Bar Harbor. Fox eloped with Harriet Biddle at the time of the Philadelphia Centennial. He came to Bar Harbor in 1875 and later built the Malvern Hotel and its cottages on Kebo Street. He was his own architect for the apartment-office building shown here. Built in 1887–88, it stood on Kebo Street opposite Mount Desert Street. Fox found himself in financial trouble after he started to build the Eden Swimming Pool Club in 1892. The project was abandoned after Fox went into bankruptcy. Talleyrand burned in 1947.

Devon

This cottage, by Rotch & Tilden, stood on Eagle Lake Road from 1888 until the fire of 1947. Among its owners were H. C. Wilkins and Harold Peabody.

Tanglewold

This DeGrasse Fox cottage stood on Kebo Street out toward Cromwell Harbor Road. It was built in 1888 and bought by Alfred M. Coats of Providence, Rhode Island in 1906. Later, A. Murray Young occupied it from 1917. Tanglewold burned in 1947.

Van Doren Cottage

Designed by William Poindexter & Co. of Washington, this Hulls Cove cottage, was built in 1887–88 for Mary Van Doren. It was later owned by Julia and Guy Whiting of Washington. It survived the 1947 fire but was demolished in 1969.

Ban-y-Byrn

Architect S. V. Stratton designed this Norman Road cottage, which was built in 1888–89, for Albert Clifford Barney of Cincinnati and Washington, D.C. Barney was president of the Barney Railroad Car Foundry.

His wife was Alice Pike Barney, daughter of the owner of Pike's Opera House. Alice Barney studied under artists Carolus Duran and James Whistler in Paris; her paintings were exhibited at the Corcoran Gallery in Washington. She was also a sculptor, playwright, and patron of the arts. She founded the Neighborhood House in Washington for the needy and the unfortunate and invented a method for blending and dyeing cloth, with the profits from this process going to the House. She was the architect and contractor for her own house — The Studio — which, together with its art treasures, was left to the City of Washington after her death in 1931.

Not least, the liberal Alice Barney was the mother of the legendary Natalie Barney, to whom Remy de Gourmont addressed his *Letters to the Amazon*. Natalie Barney's biographer finds it significant that one of the Maine Central ferryboats that took the Barneys to Bar Harbor was named the *Sappho*.

From 1930, Ban-Y-Byrn was owned by Joseph Wholean. It burned in the 1947 fire.

Strawberry Hill

This cottage, by Rotch & Tilden, was built in 1889 for J. Frederick May of Washington, D.C., and was later owned by George Munson of Philadelphia. Until the 1947 fire, it stood on Strawberry Hill.

Kenarden Lodge

Designed by Rowe and Baker of New York City, this imposing cottage was built on the shore path in 1892 for John S. Kennedy at a cost of $200,000 — a tremendous sum in those days. It had its own electric power plant.

John Stewart Kennedy was a Scotsman who never lost his brogue. After a short business stay in America he returned, became a partner of Bar Harbor summer resident Morris K. Jesup, and founded his own banking house, J. S. Kennedy & Co. He was important in railroad building, particularly western railroads, and was usually referred to in the contemporary press as the "railroad king." At his death in 1909, he was a major stockholder in the Northern Pacific and Great Northern railroads. A philanthropist and active supporter of organized charity, Kennedy has a prominent place, along with Charles Eliot and John D. Rockefeller, Jr., in the Mount Desert hagiology. On his deathbed, he is said to have whispered to his wife: "Remember . . . that I promised Mr. Dorr . . . to help him get that land." Like his friend Jesup, who organized the New York Society for the Suppression of Vice, Kennedy was one of a group of moral entrepreneurs who organized a committee of "Christian millionaires." He was famous in Bar Harbor for snouting out card games in an effort to cleanse the village of its "gambling hells."

The next grandee to occupy Kenarden Lodge was Dr. John Thompson Dorrance, a chemist who joined the Campbell Company in 1897 and invented condensed soup. By 1904 they were selling sixteen million cans a year. When Dorrance died in 1930, after having been president of Campbell since 1914, he left the third largest estate recorded up to then: $115 million.

Kenarden Lodge was torn down in 1960. A new cottage was built on the site in the 1970s by Dorrance's grandson Tristram Colket.

"You will recall the character around town, Jim Foley. Known to all the summer colony, as they engaged his cut-under to go to parties, for he entertained them with stories and gossip, both local and the summer colony. One time when the elder J. P. Morgan was here on the Corsair, *he engaged Foley to drive him one afternoon to John S. Kennedy's estate on the Shore Path. Foley knew that Mr. Kennedy took a nap in the afternoon and as he so often drove him, he told Foley that he was never to be disturbed in the afternoon. But Foley, wanting to earn his fare, took him as far as the gate house and then told J. P. that that was as far as he could take him and the reasons for same. The Old Man became indignant, said that Mr. Kennedy would see him, and to drive to the main entrance. Foley refused and J. P. had to return uptown and phone Mr. Kennedy, was let in, and said to Mr. Kennedy that was the first time in his life that he never had his own way. Foley had said, by the way, that he didn't give a damn who Morgan was, he knew Kennedy and he had his instructions."*

— Chester Wescott

Birnam

This cottage, by Rotch & Tilden, occupied a considerable estate on Highbrook Road. Built in 1892–93 for Charles Fry of Manchester, Massachusetts, it was demolished about 1945.

Corfield

Another design by Boston's Rotch & Tilden, this Eden Street house was built in 1893 for Mrs. George P. Bowler of Cincinnati. Its next occupant, from 1922, was William Cooper Procter, the soap manufacturer, who ran Procter & Gamble until 1930. Already famous for Ivory — the first soap to float — the firm developed Crisco and a now-forgotten art form, soap sculpture, during Procter's tenure. Procter assured himself a place in the history books when his conditional gift of $500,000 to Princeton for an isolated graduate school precipitated an epic holy war pitting Woodrow Wilson, then president of Princeton, against the dominion and arrogance of wealth. Procter withdrew his offer. Wilson emerged from the battle 99 44/100% pure and went into politics.

Corfield was torn down about 1965.

Donaque

," Bar Harbor, Me.

This cottage stood on Cleftstone Road and was built in 1893–94 for A. Howard Hinckle of Cincinnati from the design of Boston architects Andrews, Jaques & Rantoul. Hinckle, publisher and patron of the arts, died in 1911. Three years later, Hinckle's widow was a participant in one of the most notable events in Bar Harbor history.

In August 1914, with war imminent, the North German Lloyd liner *Kronprinzessin Cecilie*, bound for the fatherland with 1,216 passengers (including Mrs. Hinckle and her daughter) and $13 million in gold bullion, received orders to avoid Allied shipping and seek a secure haven. Her skipper, Captain Charles Pollak, put into Bar Harbor. Thus it was that as dawn broke on August 4, 1914, Mrs. Hinckle and her daughter, thinking at first that they were nearing the Azores, gradually discerned the outlines of their own Bar Harbor cottage, and they began to weep copiously.* Another Bar Harbor passenger, C. Ledyard Blair, piloted the ship into Frenchman Bay, where she remained until November. Eventually she became the troop transport *Mount Vernon*.

Donaque was demolished about 1939.

---

*According to Cleveland Amory, the sisters also discerned their servants out on the lawn at the end of what was obviously an all-night champagne party celebrating their departure.

Elsinore

Adjacent to the Hinckle cottage on Cleftstone Road stood this handsome cottage by Andrews, Jaques & Rantoul. It was built in 1893–94 for Hugh McMillan of Detroit.

The next occupant of Elsinore was Mrs. Henry F. Dimock of New York, Boston, and Washington. She was the sister of William C. Whitney, Cleveland's Secretary of the Navy, New York street railway magnate, and owner of one of America's great racing stables. Of Whitney it has been written that he was one of the few men of real education, cultivation, and intellectual charm to achieve social success in his generation. Whitney was briefly a Bar Harbor summer resident; his sister was one of the oldest — she lived to be ninety-seven — and one of the best loved.

Susan Whitney married Henry Farnum Dimock, a financier as well as director and/or president of many large corporations, including the Yale Corporation, the Boston & Maine Railroad, and the Dominion Coal Company. Her Bar Harbor home was a center of hospitality not only for gatherings of the socially prominent summer colony but also of the year-round local residents. She gave many musicales at her home, to which Bar Harbor residents were invited. Mrs. Dimock was also one of the founders and chief supporters of Bar Harbor's Building of Arts.

Elsinore was demolished about 1945.

Baymeath

Boston architects Andrews, Jaques & Rantoul designed this attractive Colonial-style house, which was built at Hulls Cove in 1895–96.

It was the summer home for more than fifty years of Mrs. Louise DeKoven Bowen, widow of Joseph T. Bowen, a Chicago banker. Mrs. Bowen, said to have been the first woman in Chicago to drive behind her own coachmen in livery, was a strong-minded woman with intense social sympathies. She was a member of many philanthropic, civic, and social organizations and was an early activist in the women's suffrage movement. She is best remembered for her association with Hull House, which she joined in 1893 at the suggestion of her close friend (and Hulls Cove neighbor) Jane Addams. She was president of Hull House for seven years, contributing much energy and money, and continued as treasurer of the center until 1953, shortly before her death at age ninety-four.

Baymeath was razed in 1979.

Honfleur

Another Hulls Cove cottage was Honfleur, named after the French port from whence sailed the Jesuit mission ship *Jonas* in 1613 to the harbor that they named Saint Sauveur (probably Cromwell or Compass Harbor). Honfleur was designed by John Clark and built in 1896 for Herbert Parsons of New York. It was later owned by the elegant and urbane Sumner Welles (1892–1961), Under-Secretary of State from 1943 to 1947, who is still remembered fondly by many Bar Harbor natives. Honfleur was demolished in 1964.

Llangollen

This cottage, built in 1896, was owned by Charles Jackson; Mrs. Jackson's daughter, Mrs. William Blake; then Mrs. Duer Baker; and finally by Prince Mahmet Burhaneddin of Turkey. It stood on Eagle Lake Road and burned in the 1947 fire.

Keewaydin

This lower Main Street cottage, by the well-known firm of Lamb & Rich of New York, was built in 1898 for New York banker Gardiner Sherman. It burned in 1947.

Hare Forest

Built in 1899–1900 for L.N. Kettle, who called it Ledge Cliff, this cottage was purchased in 1926 by the *second* Potter Palmer, who changed the name. Potter Palmer II, president of the Art Institute of Chicago, lived until 1943. Mrs. Potter Palmer II lived on to become one of Bar Harbor's *grandes dames*. Hare Forest was on Schooner Head Road, directly in the path of the 1947 fire.

Glen Eyrie

This Eden Street house was built in 1902 by U.S. Senator John B. Henderson of Missouri. Henderson was an active member of the Senate during the Civil War and Reconstruction period. Although he favored the renomination of Hannibal Hamlin to the vice-presidency in 1865, he and William Pitt Fessenden were leaders of the opposition to impeachment of President Andrew Johnson. A former slaveholder, he was true to the Union and wrote and introduced the 13th Amendment abolishing slavery.

Glen Eyrie was torn down about 1933.

Islescote

The site of this cottage was Ogden Point, just south of Pointe d'Acadie, whose owner George Vanderbilt built Islescote for his sister, Mrs. William Jay Schieffelin, in 1902. Cleveland Amory presents a charming picture of the Schieffelin family riding out in the morning, eleven strong on eleven black mounts, each of the nine Schieffelin children stepping down on smaller and smaller ponies, with the last on a tiny black Shetland.

The house was designed by architect A. W. Longfellow and was demolished in 1940.

Pinchot Cottage

Built in 1903 by the tall, fastidious Amos Pinchot (1873–1944), New York lawyer and brother of Gifford, friend and later foe of Franklin Roosevelt, and a man who fought both big business *and* big government. Other occupants were Mrs. Howard O. Sturges of Providence, Rhode Island; Mrs. Rush Sturges; and Elizabeth Hudson. The cottage stood on Eden Street and burned in the 1947 fire.

Sonogee

One of Bar Harbor's most famous summer cottages was this Eden Street house. It was built in 1903 for Henry Lane Eno (1871–1928), poet and author and research associate in psychology at Princeton. This remarkable man was also an expert on birds and was appointed chief ornithologist at Lafayette (Acadia) National Park in 1919.

The most famous occupant of Sonogee was A. Atwater Kent, a self-made man whose extravagant ways came to symbolize the era of the 1920s. Born in Burlington, Vermont, young Kent manifested his precocity by taking out his first patent — for an electric top — at the age of ten. In the early 1900s he was producing electrical systems for automobiles, and in 1923 he began building radios. A diminutive man, he was affable but quirky. In an interview with a *Time* reporter he said he wished to enjoy "the simple life on a grand scale." His parties are legendary — three orchestras, thousands of guests, launches carrying guests back and forth to the Kent yacht. Nothing like it was seen before in Bar Harbor — nor, it goes without saying, since.

Kent's company suffered during the depression, and in 1937 he rid himself of everything — businesses, estates, and wife — and moved to Bel Air, California, where he continued to entertain on a lavish scale. When he died in 1949, his estate had dwindled to $8 million, much of which he left to his new-found Hollywood friends.

Sonogee, minus its second story and with two wings added, became a nursing facility in 1976.

Wingwood House

In 1925 the E. T. Stotesburys arrived in Bar Harbor and bought the Frenchman Bay cottage of A. J. Cassatt. Mrs. Stotesbury took one look around, called in the architects Magaziner, Eberhard & Harris, and promptly set about remodeling. The result of their labors, at a cost of $1.1 million, was Wingwood House, an eighty-room "cottage" with a thirty-room servants' wing. The house was heated by fifty-six electric wall heaters, five hot air furnaces, and twenty-six hand-carved marble fireplaces imported from Europe. There were twenty-eight bathrooms, and fifty-two telephones plus twenty-three extensions. A landscape gardener was called in to move a hundred big pine trees from here to there and plant ten elms at a cost of $1,500 an elm.

The dapper and genial Stotesbury, whose nickname was "Little Sunshine," went to work at the age of twelve as a $16.60-a-month clerk with the Philadelphia banking house of Drexel & Company. Eventually, he became a senior partner in both Drexel and J. P. Morgan & Company. He never retired. On the day he died in 1938, at the age of ninety, he put in a full workday at Drexel.

Stories about Mrs. Stotesbury are legion. She shifted her plants around the grounds twice a week, maintained a full-time fashion designer and costume secretary, once organized a half-million-dollar alligator safari to provide leather for a set of matching luggage, and explained that the gold fixtures in her bathroom were an economy, for "they saved polishing, you know." After her death in 1946, she was remembered fondly as a perfect hostess "who made every guest feel as if he or she were the only one invited." Who could ask for a better epitaph?

Alexander J. Cassatt, whose Four Acres, by Chapman & Fraser of Boston, occupied the site from 1903, was a Philadelphian born into wealth. He became a civil engineer, joined the Pennsylvania Railroad, retired in 1882, and returned in 1899 as president. Perhaps his greatest monument was New York's lost and lamented Pennsylvania Terminal, which was begun in 1906, the year of his death.

Wingwood stood in disrepair until 1953, when it was demolished to make way for the Canadian National *Bluenose* ferry terminal.

Woodlands

This cottage, by Irving John Gill,* sited on lower Main Street, was built in 1903–04 for New York lawyer Louis B. McCagg. Later it was the home of Mrs. William Moore, the former Edith Pulitzer, daughter of the newspaper wizard and great-granddaughter-in-law of the man who wrote the ballad *A Visit from Saint Nicholas.*

The house burned in 1947.

---

*Irving John Gill (1870–1936) was to become one of the most important pioneers of the modern architectural movement. His special interest was low-cost housing.

The Bungalow

This cottage, by Paul Hunt, stood on Bar Island from 1907 until 1943, when it was destroyed by fire. It was built for Mrs. Hunt Slater of Washington, D.C., and later occupied by her nephew Hunt Diederick.

Bar Island is actually in the town of Gouldsboro, but it is part of the Bar Harbor scene.

Archbold Cottage

In 1904 Ed Mears built this cottage, which burned in the 1947 fire, for Ann Archbold. It stood on Cleftstone Road, just north of Eagle Lake Road.

Ms. Archbold, who reverted to her maiden name after divorcing her British husband, was the daughter of a Standard Oil Company president, who, according to Lucius Beebe, "strove valiantly to stem the flow of spending money deriving from Standard Oil from going down the rat hole of good works." An artist, she traveled and studied in Europe. The idea for the cottage came from travels in Italy. In Paris she had a model made of her proposed villa. An unusual feature of her cottage was the "vanishing table," a round table supported in the center by a hollow drum through which a dumbwaiter brought up the meal, delivering it on a traveling disk that became flush with the top of the table. This novel arrangement was said to have been designed to outwit the blackmailing Colonel William D'Alton Mann, publisher of the scandal-mongering *Town Topics*, who planted spies among the domestic staff of his wealthy targets. Another summer resident, Arthur Train, made Ms. Archbold's life the subject of his novel *His Children's Children*.

Greenway Court

Greenway Court, by Howland Jones of Andrews, Jaques & Rantoul, was built by Francis Burton Harrison in 1910. It stood on a thickly wooded hill above lower Main Street overlooking the harbor. Harrison was appointed Governor General of the Philippines, and in the summer of 1914 the house was occupied by Louise and Warner Leeds of New York. It became the setting that season for an extraordinary party.

After changes had been rung on almost every method of entertainment for the amusement of Society, Louise Leeds sent out invitations for a costume ball to be known as "Au Fond de la Mer." Two-thirds of the summer colony (according to the New York *Herald*) were requested to come in the attire of "mythical or actual denizens" of the bottom of the sea. Although her timing, as will be seen, was unfortunate, the party was held August 10.

When the carriages arrived at Greenway Court, the excited guests were herded through a simulated grotto to what was ordinarily the front entrance of the cottage. Here they were met by an attendant dressed as a lobster, who announced their names and pointed the way to the lawn, where Mr. and Mrs. Leeds, dressed as Poseidon and Amphitrite, and attended by a group of Nereids, welcomed the revelers to a "veritable fairyland." Myriads of green, purple, and blue lights were hidden behind a green covering. Seaweed, shells, stones, and piles of rock were strewn about the lawn and "fishy-looking objects" moved about in the dim light. An entertainment followed, including a lobster quadrille, after which there was a supper inside the house.

Most of the guests arrived shortly after 10 P.M., when a trumpet call was heard out at sea. It came from the yacht *The Duchess*, anchored offshore, but a thick fog hid the boat with its green lights representing a phantom ship. There was an echo from the wooded hills, and then among the rocks was heard the Valkyrie call from Wagner. In the distance below was heard ringing, which, as it approached, appeared to be a chorus of sailors singing selections from *The Flying Dutchman.*

As might be expected, mermaids draped with pearls and coral were redundant. Others showed more imagination. "Mrs. A. Wells tried to look like a sponge."

Apparently one of Colonel William D'Alton Mann's local spies was concealed in the seaweed, perhaps disguised as a shark. The next issue of *Town Topics* took a sour view of the festivities:

"It seemed rather unfortunate that Louise Leeds should have given her circus at Bar Harbor in the shadow of the European calamity [the Great War had just begun] *and on the same day of the funeral of the wife of the nation's Chief Executive. There was in consequence a deal of criticism, and many of those who attended showed very plainly that they did not enter into the spirit of the occasion. Carriages were called before supper, and I saw Mrs. Burton Harrison, Mrs. William Jay Schieffelin, the Hall McCormicks, and others leaving about midnight. . . . Louise did postpone her ball on account of the death of Mrs. Wilson, but unsympathetic ones declared that that merely proved a convenience, as she was not ready*

for the affair and this offered an opportunity for a rehearsal to smooth over the rough places. . . . It surely took a stretch of the imagination to imagine Louise as a Greek goddess. The effort of Mrs. Fremont Smith to look like a sea nymph proved rather ludicrous. Only youth should impersonate youth. . . . Many questioned the taste of De Witt Parshall, who went to the Leeds ball as a drowning man. As Death under a robe trimmed with sea products he was more repulsive than attractive."

Nevertheless, the *Herald,* which never missed a chance to publicize and mock Society, called it the "most brilliant event of the season," which seems to confirm Harry Lehr's cynical verdict of Society: "I saw that most human beings are fools, and that the best way to live harmoniously with them and make them like you is to pander to their stupidity. They want to be entertained, to be made to laugh. They will overlook almost anything so long as you amuse them."

Perhaps Mrs. Leeds realized that the Bar Harbor of "plain living and high thinking" was coming to an end, that dignity and good taste were becoming obsolete. In any event, the sophisticated absurdity of "Au Fond de la Mer" was a harbinger of the Stotesbury-Kent era to come.

Greenway Court burned to the ground in October 1947.

Fairview

This Eden Street cottage, by Andrews, Jaques & Rantoul of Boston, was built in 1909 for "Commodore" Philip Livingston. A later occupant was author and playwright Mary Roberts Rinehart, whose cleverly plotted books deal often with murder and horror but are leavened with humor and wit. Mrs. Rinehart, whose own chef once tried to kill her, was burned out in 1947.

Buonriposo

This cottage, which stood on Eden Street, was designed and built in 1904 by Ernesto Fabbri, who lived there with his brother Alessandro.

Alessandro Fabbri was a research associate in physiology at the American Museum of Natural History in New York. He was also an amateur radio operator who set up an experimental station at Otter Cliffs. He was the first to achieve 24-hour radio contact with European stations. When World War I broke out, he offered his station to the Navy, which enlarged it, set up direct wires to Washington, and conducted most of its European traffic with the benefit of the radio reflection from the hills of Mount Desert. In 1920 Lieutenant Fabbri received the Navy Cross for his contributions to the war effort.

Alessandro Fabbri, who never married, died in 1922. In 1935 the former radio station was moved to the Schoodic Peninsula. His friends erected a monument to him at the parking area at Otter Point on the Ocean Drive just opposite the former station. His friend Arthur Train read the dedication and said, "Perhaps his most conspicuous and endearing trait was his capacity for friendship."

The house burned in 1918, was rebuilt in 1919, and finally torn down in 1963.

LEFT TO RIGHT: *LYNAM HOUSE, ST. SAUVEUR, WEST END HOTEL, BIRCH TREE INN, RODICK HOUSE, GRAND CENTRAL*
(**CIRCA** *1882)*

Hotels and
Guest Houses

Agamont House

The Agamont House was Bar Harbor's first hotel. It was built by Tobias Roberts, a sometime shopkeeper, postmaster, and visionary. Roberts was the first to realize the possibilities of catering to tourists and later built a crude wharf to land potential guests who until then had to make an overland journey from Southwest Harbor. The Agamont stood on the rise on Main Street, across from the present Agamont Park. It burned in 1888.

Hamor House

Captain James Hamor's house
was built in 1864. It stood near the
corner of Cottage and Main streets.

Rodick House

In 1866 David Rodick built a small guest house on the northern slope of what was then known as "Captain Hamor's Ridge" (Main Street at Rodick Place). The house prospered, managed to overcome bad publicity resulting from an outbreak of scarlet fever, and in 1875 expanded to accommodate 275 guests, making it the largest hotel in Bar Harbor.

Applications for rooms continued to multiply until rooms had to be reserved two years in advance. Turning away would-be customers was a source of grief for the enterprising Rodicks, who decided that the hotel must be enlarged again. Local architect and builder John Clark was called in, and Clark planned an extension to begin at the northern end of the old section, continue parallel with Main Street for forty-five feet, and then bend westward for 225 feet.

On November 14, 1881, seventy carpenters employed by master builder E. T. Winwood began to work. The result, nine months later, was the impressive six-story pile shown here. Advertised as the largest hotel in Maine, it had 400 rooms (but no private bathrooms), a dining room able to serve a thousand guests,* and a 25-foot-wide piazza running along the front and one of the sides of the hotel for a distance of 500 feet.

The Rodick House soon became one of the most famous society hotels in America — fully the equal of such famed hostelries as Saratoga's Grand Union, but less formal. Dances were held twice a week, and there was undoubtedly good conversation on the piazza, but the chief attraction of the place was the lobby, which became an arena for dalliance known as the "Fish Pond." (For some reason chaperones were less vigilant in Bar Harbor than at other watering places.)

But the hotel era even then was beginning its decline, and while age and tradition have their special charms, they can be carried too far in a hotel, especially one in which the latest advances in indoor plumbing have been ignored. By the early 1890s, the Rodick, then leased by A. W. Bee, had a look of melancholy decay. It closed briefly in 1892 and 1894, but staggered on for a few more years and was demolished in 1906.

---

*But they weren't served well, according to Charles Dudley Warner and F. Marion Crawford. One of Warner's fictional characters says, "You musn't judge of the variety here by the table at Rodick's." For the epicurean Crawford, "Biscuits and preserves formed an appreciable part of every traveler's luggage."

RODICK HOUSE, 1866

RODICK HOUSE, 1875

RODICK HOUSE, 1882

Newport Hotel

The select Newport was built
in 1869 on a site just south of the
present-day Agamont Park, near the
parking area. It was demolished in
1938.

Ocean House

One of Bar Harbor's many "dainty and refined" hotels, the Ocean House holds the record for longevity. Built in 1870, it stood in the Field until 1973.

Newport Hotel

The select Newport was built in 1869 on a site just south of the present-day Agamont Park, near the parking area. It was demolished in 1938.

THE SECOND ATLANTIC HOUSE, RENAMED THE LOUISBURG IN 1887

the modern French style and finish, surmounted by a large observatory." In 1887 it was purchased by a Miss M. L. Balch and named the Louisburg (after Louisburg Square, Boston), which is shown here. Miss Balch added a tennis court and a music room where the Louisburg Orchestra, "composed of eminent artists," gave concerts morning and evening.

After Miss Balch's death, the hotel was leased, in 1911 to J. A. Sherrad and for two years to L. C. Prior, proprietor of the Lennox Hotel in Boston. In 1916 the Misses Healey of Saratoga Springs ran it. It became the Lorraine when purchased by the Lafayette Hotel Corporation in 1921, and it managed, incredibly, to stay afloat until 1939, when it was leveled and the property was divided into house lots.

Rockaway

Another small hotel built in 1870 was Tobias L. Roberts's Rockaway, which stood near the Maine Central wharf on the eastern side of the present-day Agamont Park. It was torn down about 1916.

St. Sauveur

Another hotel that went up in 1870 was the St. Sauveur, designed by John Clark of Bar Harbor and owned by Fred A. Alley. An annex was added in 1880. The hotel burned in 1881 but was rebuilt the following year. A contemporary guidebook says the St. Sauveur "enjoys the patronage of a very smart set of guests." Furthermore, its situation on Mount Desert Street, Bar Harbor's "most popular boulevard," gave it "the distinction of being entirely free from objectionable surroundings." It was demolished in 1945.

Grand Central

Built by Asa Hodgkins in 1873, the Grand Central stood until 1899, when it was purchased by the town for $45,000 from Johnston Livingston, who had purchased the hotel in 1892. The Grand Central stood on the site of the present-day Village Green.

The Grand Central grew from the small Bay View, which the Messrs. Hamor and Young built on the site in 1868. All went well until 1873, when Bar Harbor was confronted with the first serious threat to its growing resort business. Henry Walton Swift, who apparently saw the humorous side of everything, versified:

One night, when laugh and gay reply
  abounded,
And loud with mirth the Bay View's
  walls resounded,
The doctors, in a muffled
  conversation,
About their troubles held a
  consultation,
But listeners keen, by anxious terror
  stirred,
The words of evil omen overheard.

The "words of evil omen" were eight cases of typhoid fever (five more were to break out later). The news quickly spread to the Boston and New York newspapers, and beyond, that Bar Harbor was a fever-infested town!

It was found that only one well was infected, and action was taken promptly. Surface drainage was diverted into cesspools or into sewers leading into the ocean. A *constant stream of running water* (the italics are from a Rodick House advertisement) was brought in from Eagle Lake in wooden troughs constructed by the erstwhile ship carpenters of Eden, and a scholarly article by Dr. W. J. Morton, "Mount Desert and Typhoid Fever," was reprinted from the *Boston Medical and Surgical Journal* and circulated as a pamphlet. The world outside was reassured, and all was well for the opening of the 1874 season.

On July 4, 1874, a seventeen-piece band helped to celebrate the diversion of Eagle Lake water to the town.

Belmont Hotel

The Belmont was built in
1879 near the corner of Mount Desert
and Kebo Streets, then the outskirts of
town. Like its neighbor, the Malvern,
it burned in October 1947.

West End

Built in 1878–79, the large, wooden stick-style West End was, in Vincent Scully's words, "a great barn, rough, boisterous and warm" in its colors of Indian red, brown, and olive green, colors typical of the cottage architecture of the period. The hotel, which stood on West Street, grew to accommodate 400 guests, second in size only to the Rodick. It was torn down in 1900.

Hotel Des Isles

The hotel Des Isles, built in 1881, stood on Newton Way, just off Main Street. It was renamed the Maine Central Hotel in 1897 but was torn down only three years later. The original name, incidentally, was generally pronounced "Desizzle." Later the family gave in and anglicized their name thus.

Marlborough

In 1882, Charles Higgins erected the Marlborough on Main Street opposite Cottage Street. He moved the Deering House, Bar Harbor's second-oldest hotel, which had occupied the site, but retained it as an annex. Sold to Martin Roberts in 1905, the Marlborough itself became an annex of the Newport.

Malvern Hotel

By the 1890s the cottage era was in full bloom and most of the older and larger hotels were obsolete and declining. There were a few, however, of such dignity and social standing that they continued to prosper. Among the latter was the Malvern on Kebo Street, built in 1882 by DeGrasse Fox. Connected with the Malvern were eleven "cottages," some with as many as fourteen rooms, six baths, and two sitting rooms.

After Fox became bankrupt, the hotel was purchased by Mrs. Morris Jesup in 1910 for $50,000. The following year it was bought by Thomas De Witt Cuyler, and in 1924 by the Malvern Hotel Company, Inc., a firm formed by a gang of summer residents including William Procter, the floating soap manufacturer, and Beatrix Farrand, the landscape gardener. It was sold to Chester Wescott in 1930 and burned in 1947.

The Porcupine

The Porcupine was built in 1887 on Main Street opposite Mount Desert Street. Its proud boast was "bathrooms on every floor." In 1906 it was purchased by Miss T. E. Martin, who renamed it the New Florence, after her previous hostelry. Sold again in 1917, it burned the following year.

DeGregoire Hotel

In 1892 DeGrasse Fox made plans for a structure to be known as the Eden Swimming Pool Club, but by 1895 Fox had gone into bankruptcy and the land and an unfinished building were sold at public auction. Fox's plans were abandoned. It became the property of local contractor George Wescott, who sold it to W. R. Lee. Lee added a wing and opened it as an apartment hotel in 1907. The DeGregoire was sited by Eddy's Brook (Eden Street, corner of West Street). It burned in the 1947 fire.

The DeGregoire was named after Mme. Marie Thérèse de la Mothe Cadillac de Grégoire, granddaughter of Sieur Antoine de la Mothe Cadillac, French fur trader, colonial administrator, and founder of Detroit.* Cadillacs have been coming to Mount Desert ever since.

*In 1784 Mme. de Grégoire laid claim to her seigneurie at Mount Desert. A bewildering series of events followed, involving Thomas Jefferson, Samuel Adams, the Marquis de Lafayette, General Henry Knox, and many, many others. (*See* R. W. Hale, *The Story of Bar Harbor*. New York: Ives Washburn, 1949, pp. 88*ff*.).

THE BAR HARBOR SWIMMING CLUB

Civic Sites
and Structures

Bar Harbor Swimming Club

Built in 1903, and designed by Andrews, Jaques & Rantoul, the original club featured a saltwater pool blocked off in the bay, a bath house and reception room, private dressing rooms, and two tennis courts. In time, these primitive facilities became a source of embarrassment, and in 1929–30 they were replaced with the present Bar Harbor Club.

Building of Arts

Designed by Guy Lowell and with the financial support of Mrs. Henry Dimock, Mrs. Robert Abbe, Henry Lane Eno, George Dorr, and George Vanderbilt, the severely classic Building of Arts was dedicated July 13, 1907, with a concert featuring Emma Eames. Owen Johnson wandered about the grounds and wrote: "One listens for the echoes of a shepherd's pipe or seeks among the tree-trunks the flitting passage of a flying robe." Another observer, looking down from Newport Mountain, was reminded of the temple of Theseus as seen from the Acropolis.

The Boston Symphony performed there. So did Vladimir de Pachmann and Fritz Kreisler and Paderewski and Olive Fremstad and, to come down a few pegs, Ted Shawn and José Iturbi. Nevertheless, it never realized its aim of becoming America's Bayreuth, and when the building burned to the ground in 1947, it got mixed reviews. According to Richard Hale, "Few tears were shed."

The Building of Arts stood off Cromwell Harbor Road near the corner of Kebo Street.

Mount Desert Canoe Club

Founded in 1887, the Canoe Club occupied a boathouse at the Pendleton & Roberts wharf and a clubhouse on Bob Sproul's property on Albert Meadow before finally fetching up in 1888 at the Bar Island Clubhouse shown here. A few Indians were always present to provide instruction, and receptions were held weekly during August. The Canoe Club reached its highwater mark, so to speak, about 1900, when it had over three hundred members.

The Casino

Built in 1901, the Casino stood on upper Cottage Street. It was the scene of graduation exercises, basketball games, town meetings, summer theatre, and an orgy called the "Way Bak Ball." One of the big events of the summer was the Hospital Benefit Ball. Chester Wescott, who had a keen eye for the nuances of social discrimination, recalled that "all of the natives would stand out on the sidewalk and see the carriages called out at the end of the performance. *They* did not like the peasants watching them, so they suggested to Mrs. Dimock that they build the Building of Arts." The Casino managed without *them* until it was finally torn down in 1970.

Jordan Pond House

This is an early view of the Jordan Pond House, still famous for tea and popovers, but not, alas, in this building, which burned to the ground in 1979. Occupying a site popular for years as a location for picnics, it was converted from farmhouse to tea house in 1896.

---

*The Jordan Pond House is, of course, in Seal Harbor, not in Bar Harbor. But never mind; it was, and is, bound up with the life of every Bar Harborite.

Kebo Valley Club House

The founders of the Kebo Valley Club, among whom were Charles T. How and DeGrasse Fox, had no thought of golf. The original Kebo Valley Club House shown here housed a pretty little theatre and a restaurant. The grounds included a race track, a baseball field, and several lawn tennis and croquet lawns. The club house was formally opened on July 18, 1889. It burned in 1899 but was rebuilt the following year. The first "golf ground" — a six-hole course — was built in 1892. By 1896 nine holes were in operation, and in 1916 the club bought land to make up a second nine holes.

The second club house burned in the 1947 fire, but a third was built in time for the 1948 season. No longer the preserve of the wealthy summer resident, today members of the proletariat may be seen there trying to propel a small ball with the use of a club into a hole with as few strokes as possible.

Oasis Club / Mount Desert Reading Room

Bar Harbor's first social club began in 1874 when a group of men from the summer colony rented a small house on the corner of School and Mount Desert Streets; it was called the Oasis Club. Here the members could prime themselves with cocktails in defiance of Maine's prohibition law.

In 1881 the club moved to the Veazie Cottage on the shore near Birch Point and incorporated as the Mount Desert Reading Room, with the avowed purpose, as stated in the charter, of promoting "literary and social culture." The club prospered, the Veazie Cottage was hauled away to another location, and a splendid new building, designed by William Ralph Emerson, was erected on the site in 1887. After an earlier pier had been washed away in a storm, a massive steel pier replaced it. This structure became a famous Bar Harbor landmark and was pictured in guidebooks, brochures, and postcards until its demolition in the 1930s.

The Reading Room became *the* center of social activities during the summers before World War I. In 1910, President William H. Taft was welcomed there upon his arrival in the village.

After the war, membership fell off sharply. Members of the summer colony were now defying na-

tional prohibition in their own cottages. By 1922, the Reading Room, which had opened with 415 subscribers, was down to ten members — which probably made it the most exclusive club in America. In its last year, all would-be members were blackballed.

The clubhouse and pier were sold to the Maine Central Railroad, which leased them to the Bar Harbor Yacht Club in 1924. The Yacht Club went by the boards in 1932, but the following year the building was resurrected when a group of hotel owners organized the Shore Club for the use of their guests. During World War II the U. S. Navy leased the building. It was sold to the Bar Harbor Hotel Corporation in 1948, and reopened in 1950, somewhat altered and with a wing added, as the Bar Harbor Hotel.

It is now called the Bar Harbor Motor Inn.

Robin Hood Park

The park was owned by Colonel Edward Morrell of Philadelphia, an avid horseman. In 1900 he made the grounds available to the newly founded Horse Show and Fair Association. Horse shows were held there for three days during the last week in August from 1900 to 1912. Chester Wescott recalls the horse show days:

"All the socialites from Newport, Southampton, Lenox, and the North Shore came to this event. The boxes, which only contained eight folding chairs, were sold for the three-day period for $500 to finance the event. Ed McLean, who had purchased the Montgomery Sears estate on the shore path, got the idea into his head that he would put a few of the old-timers like Philip Livingston, Colonel Morrell, Ketterlinus, Pulitzers, and a few others who always walked away with the blue ribbons, to shame. He sent over to England and purchased the finest horseflesh possible. Entered them. He had a big tent just behind the grandstand and I recall riding down to the Robin Hood Park in a cart with at least twenty-four cases of beer for his attendants. It was really something to see. He engaged Eleonora Sears and Dorothy Forbes from Boston to drive with him. Believe it or not, every time they appeared before the judges' stand, Ed won all the blue ribbons. He would tip that old felt hat he wore in acknowledgment, which was rather amusing to the spectators."

"Another Horse Show story: Mr. Pineo was in charge of the Horse Show. David Rodick was his nephew and helped him with his duties. I remember one day they were making up the program and Pineo was going to put Edsel Ford's children and the Rockefeller children with their pony carriages in the same class. In competition. Dave immediately shouted, 'You're crazy, don't do that! Put them in separate classes, so that each can get a blue ribbon and cup. We need their box money to finance this show and you will ruin everything.' This was done and everyone was happy."

119

BAR HARBOR, LOOKING EAST ON MT. DESERT STREET FROM SCOTT'S HILL, LATER CALLED HAMILTON'S HILL (1880s)

Selected
Bibliography

Index

Index